Jesus
in
The Quran

Jesus in The Quran

ALI SHAWKAT

Published by
KENANGA PERMAI SDN. BHD. (554903-T)
Unit B1-07, PJ Industrial Park,
Jalan Kemajuan,
46200 Petaling Jaya,
Selangor Darul Ehsan,
Malaysia.
Tel.: 603-7956 4127 Fax.: 603-7958 1943
E-mail: *kenper@tm.net.my*

ISBN 983-2965-17-9

Printed in Malaysia

CONTENTS

INTRODUCTION

JESUS IS A UNIQUE FIGURE IN HUMAN HISTORY. His words and deeds inspire many, and his life continues to fascinate and raise questions. So, it comes as no surprise that The Quran, the Muslim Scripture, has a lot to say about Jesus and his mother. The Quran tells the story of the conception and birth of Jesus and the difficulty Mary went through; it affirms Jesus' many miracles, summarizes his mission and call to God, refers to and praises the disciples, discusses the plot to kill Jesus and his ascension, and alludes to his expected second coming. In fact, Jesus and his mother, Mary, are two of the main figures in The Quran, presented as examples for all to follow.

To introduce the reader to *Jesus in the Quran*, relevant verses have been collected without neglect of context. Then several translations were consulted, mainly *The Noble Quran* by Hilali & Khan, and *The Quran* by Saheeh International, but also Yusuf Ali, Pickthal, and Shakir. Then, several Arabic commentaries on the Quran helped revise the translation to provide better understanding of the verses and a smoother translation from the original

Arabic. These commentaries are the source of what is in brackets within the translation. Finally and where necessary, footnotes were added for further clarification.

The reader will find the titles of the chapters of the Quran in bold, followed by the verses. The chapters of the Quran are not arranged chronologically, so the Quran does not read like a history book. Rather, many events are repeated in various chapters in the Quran for their morals and lessons, or to affirm a point or bring a new one to light. Also, verses only relevant to Jesus have been collected, so the reader might feel disconnected from the chapter. If so, we recommend reading the whole chapter for the full meaning.

87. And indeed, We gave Moses the Book and sent after him a series of messengers. And We gave Jesus, the son of Mary, clear signs and supported him with the Pure Spirit (Angel Gabriel). But isn't it that whenever a messenger came to you (O children of Israel) with what you did not like, you grew arrogant? And so some you disbelieved and some you killed.

88. And they say, "Our hearts are wrapped (preventing us from understanding what you are calling us to)." Rather, God has cursed them for their rejection (of the truth), so little do they believe.[2]

---

[1] The name of this chapter is derived from a story in verses 2:67-73, involving Moses, peace be upon him, and the Israelites.

[2] They claim they do not understand God's revelation and that is why they don't follow it, but they do understand it. The reason they do not believe is their rejection of the truth, which earned them God's anger, and so He put a barrier between the truth and them. The consequence of rejecting the truth is losing the ability to recognize it or to reach it later.

89. And when a Book from God came to them confirming what they have, and before that they used to pray for victory over those who disbelieved, then when what they recognized (to be the truth) came to them, they disbelieved in it. So let the curse of God be on the disbelievers.[3]

90. Miserable is the price for which they have sold themselves, that they would disbelieve in what God has revealed out of envy that God would give from His favor to whom He wills of His servants. So they brought on themselves anger upon anger. And there is a humiliating punishment for the disbelievers.

91. And when it is said to them, "Believe in what God has revealed," they say, "We (only) believe in what was revealed to us." And they disbelieve in what came after it, although it is the truth confirming what is with them. Say, "Why then have you killed the prophets of God (that were sent to you) before, if you indeed are believers?"

---

[3] The verse refers to what the Israelites used to say to the polytheistic Arabs before Islam. Whenever they used to quarrel with them, the Israelites would threaten the Arabs that the coming of the last prophet is near, and when he comes, the Israelites will conquer the Arabs with him. But when the last prophet turned to be an Arab, which the Israelites did not expect, they rejected him though they knew that he was the promised one they were waiting for.

130. And who turns away from the religion of Abraham except one who demeans himself. And indeed, We chose him in this world, and he is among the righteous in the Hereafter.

131. When his Lord said to him, "Submit[4]," he said, "I have submitted to the Lord of the worlds."

132. And Abraham commanded this to his sons and (so did) Jacob, (saying), "O my sons, God has chosen the religion for you, so do not die except as Muslims."

133. Or were you present when death approached Jacob, when he said to his sons, "What will you worship after me?" They said, "We will worship your God and the God of your fathers, Abraham and Ishmael and Isaac, One God, and we are Muslims (in submission) to Him."

134. That was a nation that has passed away. They will receive what they have earned, and you will receive what you have earned. And you will not be asked about what they used to do.[5]

[4] The Arabic word here is "*aslem,*" a command to accept Islam. Islam is the submission to the will of God. A Muslim is one who submits to God's will.

[5] That is, the righteousness of your forefathers will not help you if you are wicked, and their wickedness will not harm you if you are righteous. Each will receive the fruit of what they sow.

135. And they say, "Be Jews or Christians, then you will be guided." Say, "Rather, (we follow) the religion of Abraham, the upright and sincere, and he was not of those who worshipped others along with God."

136. Say, "We believe in God and what has been revealed to us and what has been revealed to Abraham, Ishmael, Isaac, Jacob, and to the prophet-descendants (of Jacob), and what has been given to Moses and Jesus, and what has been given to the prophets from their Lord. We make no distinction between any of them, and we are Muslims (in submission) to Him."

137. So if they believe like what you believe, then they are guided, but if they turn away, then they are only in opposition (to God). And God will protect you from them. And He is the All-Hearing, the All-Knowing.

138. (Follow the religion that is) the coloring from God, and who is better than God in (giving) a color? And we are His worshippers.[6]

139. Say, "Do you argue with us about God while He is our Lord and your Lord? To us belong our deeds and to you your deeds. And we are sincere to Him."

140. Or do you say that Abraham, Ishmael, Isaac, Jacob and the prophet-descendants (of Jacob) were Jews or Christians? Say, "Do you know better or does God? And who is more wrong than one who conceals the knowledge he received from God? And God is not unaware of what you do."

141. That was a nation that has passed away. They will receive what they have earned, and you will receive what you have earned. And you will not be asked about what they used to do.

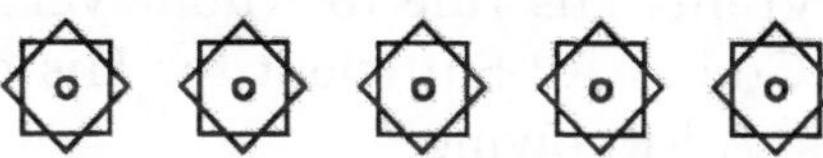

---

[6] The true religion here is like a color, it paints the human completely and transforms him until virtue becomes second nature to him. The one who does not follow the true religion will be painted by inferior human beliefs and ideologies, and the result is a flawed troubled human. Nothing is superior to God's religion, which agrees with human nature and needs. The pure uncorrupt human nature recognizes only one God as its creator, and is endowed with a general love of virtue and hatred of evil. A revealed religion from God agrees, in its assertions and demands, with that nature, and humans find comfort in that religion. Since human nature and religion both come from the same source, God, they cannot be in conflict.

246. Have you not considered the leaders of the Children of Israel after (the time of) Moses? When they said to their prophet, "Send us a king so we can fight in God's way." He said, "Maybe you will not fight, if you were commanded to fight!" They said, "Why should we not fight in God's Way while we have been driven out of our homes and our children?" But when they were commanded to fight, they turned away, except for few of them. And God is All-Aware of the wrongdoers.

247. And their prophet said to them, "God has sent you Saul as a king." They said, "How can he be a king over us when we are more worthy of that than he is, and he has not been given a lot of wealth." He said, "Indeed, God has chosen him over you and has increased him abundantly in knowledge and body (strength). God grants His rule to whomever He wills. And God is All-Sufficient for His creatures' needs, All-Knowing."

248. And their prophet said to them, "A sign of his rule is that the chest[7] will come to you, with peace and reassurance in it from your Lord, and the remains of what the house of Moses and the house of Aaron left behind, carried by the angels. This is a sign for you if you are indeed believers.

---

[7] Some translations refer to it as the Ark of the Covenant.

249. Then when Saul set out with the army, he said, "Indeed, God will test you with a river. Whoever drinks from it does not belong to me. But whoever does not taste it, he indeed belongs to me, except if one drinks a handful (of water) with his hand." But they drank from it, except for a few of them. Then when he crossed (the river) with those who believed with him, they said, "We have no power today against Goliath and his soldiers." But those who were certain that they would meet God, said, "How often has a small group overcome a large one by God's permission?" And God is with the patient.

250. And when they advanced to meet Goliath and his forces, they prayed, "Our Lord, pour upon us patience, and make our steps firm, and give us victory over the disbelieving people."

251. So they defeated them by the permission of God, and David killed Goliath, and God gave him (David) kingship and prophethood, and taught him what He willed. And if God did not push away (the harm of) one people by means of others, the earth indeed would be corrupted. And God is full of Bounty to the worlds.

252. These are the verses of God, which We recite to you (O Mohammad) in truth. And indeed, you are one of the messengers.

253. We have favored some of those messengers over others. Among them were those whom God spoke to, and He raised others in degrees, and We gave Jesus, the son of Mary, clear proofs, and We supported him with the Pure Spirit (Gabriel). And if God had wanted, those who came after them would not have fought each other after clear proofs had come to them. But they differed, and some of them believed and some of them disbelieved. And if God had wanted, they would not have fought each other, but God does what He wants[8].

---

[8] God's Will is tied to His Wisdom. So, there is wisdom in whatever God does, and there is good behind it, whether humans realize that or fail to do so because of their limitations. The verse also points to the absolute supremacy of God, where He does what He does unopposed.

CHAPTER 3 *THE FAMILY OF IMRAN*[9]

33. Indeed God chose Adam, Noah, the family of Abraham and the family of Imran over the worlds.

34. An offspring, like one another (in righteousness). And God is All-Hearing, All-Knowing.

35. (And mention) when the wife of Imran said, "O my Lord, I have vowed to You what is in my womb, to be dedicated (to Your service), so accept this from me. Indeed, You are All-Hearing, All-Knowing."

36. Then when she delivered her, she said, "O my Lord, I have delivered a female," and God knew best what she delivered, "And the male is not like the female, and I have named her Mary, and I seek refuge with You for her and for her children from Satan, the expelled (from the mercy of God)."

---

[9] Imran is Mary's father.

37. So her Lord fully accepted her, and gave her a good upbringing, and put her under the care of Zechariah. Every time Zechariah entered upon her in the prayer room, he found her supplied with food. He said, "O Mary, where do you get this from?" She said, "This is from God. Indeed, God provides for whom He wills, without limit."

38. At that time Zechariah prayed to his Lord, saying, "O my Lord, grant me from You a good child. You are indeed the Hearer of prayer."

39. Then the angels called him while he was standing in prayer in the prayer room, "Indeed, God gives you the good news of John, confirming a word from God[10], noble, chaste, and a prophet from among the righteous."

40. He said, "My Lord, how can I have a boy when I am very old, and my wife is barren?" He said, "So, God does what He wants."

---

[10] Jesus, peace be upon him, is called the word of God because he was created when God said, "Be," and he was, which is a miracle from God. Hence, because God's Word created him, Jesus is called the word of God (refer to verse 59 in this chapter). John confirmed the coming of Jesus and confirmed God's previous books and revelation, and in all this he was confirming God's Words.

41. He said, "My Lord, give me a sign." He said, "Your sign is that you will not be able to speak to people for three days except with gestures. And remember your Lord much and glorify (Him) in the afternoon and in the morning."

42. And (mention) when the angels said, "O Mary, indeed God has chosen you, purified you, and chosen you above the women of the worlds."

43. O Mary, be devoutly obedient to your Lord and prostrate and bow down along those who bow down (in prayer)."

44. This is a part of the news of the unseen, which We reveal to you (O Muhammad). You were not with them when they cast lots with their pens to (decide) which of them should take care of Mary, nor were you with them when they disputed.

45. (And mention) when the angels said, "O Mary, indeed God gives you the good news of a word from Him, whose name will be the Messiah Jesus, the son of Mary, held in honor in this world and in the Hereafter, and of those who are near to God."

46. "He will speak to the people in the cradle[11], and in old age, and he will be of the righteous."

---

[11] The details of this miracle are in verses 19:16-33.

47. She said, "My Lord, how can I have a son when no man has touched me." He said, "So (it will be,) for God creates what He wants. When He decides something, He only says to it, "Be," and it is.

48. And He will teach him the Book and wisdom and the Torah and the Gospel.

49. And (will make him) a messenger to the Children of Israel (saying), "Indeed I have come to you with a sign from your Lord. I make for you out of clay the likeness of a bird, then breathe into it, and it becomes a bird by the permission of God. And I heal the blind and the leper, and I bring the dead to life by the permission of God. And I inform you of what you eat and what you store in your houses. Surely, there is a sign for you in that, if you are believers.

50. And (I have come) confirming the Torah that was (revealed) before me, and to allow you some of what was forbidden to you. And I have come to you with a proof from your Lord, so fear God and obey me.

51. Indeed, God is my Lord and your Lord, so worship Him. This is the straight path."

52. Then when Jesus felt their (persistence in) disbelief, he said, "Who will champion with me God's (cause)?" The disciples said, "We are the champions (of the cause) of God. We believe in God, and be a witness that we are Muslims (submitting to Him).[12]

53. Our Lord, we have believed in what You have revealed, and we have followed the messenger, so write us down among the witnesses (to the truth)."

54. And they (who disbelieved) plotted, and God planned. And God is the best of the planners.

55. When God said, "O Jesus, I will take you[13] and raise you up to Me and clear you of those who disbelieve, and I will make those who follow you superior to those who disbelieve till the Day of Resurrection. Then you will all return to Me, and I will judge between you in the matters you used to disagree in."

---

[12] The name given for the disciples in the Quran is *al-Hawariyyun,* which means the purified ones, like the color white. It is also reported that they used to dress in white.

[13] Jesus was raised up in a state of sleep. The word that is used here is *wafah,* which can mean sleep or death. In Arabic, sleep is called the minor death. See also verses 6:60 and 39:42, where the word *wafah* refers to sleep and not to death. Since verse 4:157 denies the killing and crucifixion of Jesus, and since each human dies once but Jesus is supposed to come back to earth, the only remaining interpretation of the verse is sleep.

56. As for those who disbelieve, I will punish them severely in this world and in the Hereafter, and they will have no helpers.

57. And as for those who believe and do righteous deeds, He will give them their reward in full. And God does not like the wrongdoers.

58. This is what We recite to you (O Muhammad) of the verses and the wise reminder.

59. Indeed, Jesus is like Adam in front of God. He created him from dust, then said to him, "Be," and he was.[14]

60. (This is) the truth from your Lord, so be not of those who doubt.

61. Then whoever argues with you about him (Jesus) after the knowledge that has come to you, (then) say, "Come and let us call our sons and your sons, our women and your women, ourselves and yourselves, then we all pray for the curse of God to fall on those who lie."

---

[14] Adam was created when God said, "Be," and he to be without a father or a mother. And so was Jesus created by the Word of God. If the unusual birth of Jesus makes him divine, then Adam deserves more of that divinity because Jesus at least had one parent, while Adam had none. As Adam is not divine, so is Jesus not divine, but both are humble servants of God.

62. Indeed, this is the true story. And there is no deity that deserves to be worshipped except God. And indeed, God is the All-Mighty, the All-Wise.

63. But if they turn away (from accepting the truth), then indeed, God is aware of the corrupters.

64. Say, "O people of the Scripture: Come to a just statement[15] between us and you, that we worship none but God, and that we associate no partners with Him, and that none of us takes others as lords besides God[16]." But if they turn away, then say, "Be witnesses that we are Muslims (submitting to Him)."

---

[15] This is what all the prophets of God have called to and agreed upon. And so this statement is not exclusive to one group, but is the common grounds for those who want to worship God.

[16] When one obeys another human in disobedience to God, he has taken him as a lord instead of God.

CHAPTER 4 *THE WOMEN*

150. Indeed, those who disbelieve in God and His messengers and wish to separate God from His messengers (by believing in God and disbelieving in His messengers) and say, "We believe in some (messengers) but reject others," and wish to adopt a middle way between (belief and disbelief).

151. Those are truly the disbelievers. And We have prepared for the disbelievers a humiliating punishment.

152. And those who believe in God and His messengers and do not differentiate (in belief) between any of them, He will give them their rewards, and God is Ever Forgiving, Most Merciful.

153. The people of the Scripture ask you to bring them down a book from the sky (as a physical miracle confirming the truth you bring). Indeed, they had asked Moses even greater than that, when they said, "Show us God in plain sight," so the lightening struck them for their wrongdoing. Then they worshipped the calf even after clear proofs had come to them, yet We forgave that. And We gave Moses clear evidence.

154. And We raised over them the Mount for (refusing to follow) their covenant. And We said to them, "Enter the gate bowing humbly;" and We said to them, "Do not transgress on the Sabbath;" and We took from them a firm covenant; (yet all that they violated).

155. So (We cursed them) for the breaking of their covenant and their disbelief in the words of God, and for their unjust killing of the prophets, and for their saying, "Our hearts are wrapped (preventing us from understanding what you call to, so we won't follow it)." Rather, God has sealed it because of their rejection (of the truth), so little do they believe.

156. And (We cursed them) for of their disbelief and uttering against Mary a great lie (accusing her of fornication),

157. And for of their saying, "We have killed the Messiah, Jesus son of Mary, the messenger of God." But they did not kill him, nor did they crucify him, but it was made to look like him to them.[17] And those who disagree over him are in doubt (of killing) him, they have no knowledge of it except the following of guesswork, and they did not kill him for certain.

---

[17] The resemblance of Jesus was put on another, and it is he, not Jesus, who was crucified. According to several commentaries on the Quran, the one who was crucified was one of the disciples, accepting the resemblance of Jesus, and martyring himself to save Jesus in return for paradise.

158. But God raised him up to Himself.[18] And God is All-Powerful, All-Wise.

159. And there is not one of the people of the Scripture but will believe in him before his death.[19] And on the Day of Resurrection, he will be a witness against them.[20]

---

[18] Jesus was raised in body and soul, and did not die. He still lives up there, and will return towards the end of time to earth. After fulfilling his assigned role on earth, he will eventually die.

[19] The pronoun in "his death" can refer to Jesus or to the individual from the people of the Scripture. If it refers to Jesus, it means that all of the people of the Scripture will come to believe in Jesus on his second return to earth and before his death. Jesus then will confirm that he is a prophet from God, not God nor the son of God, and will ask all people to worship God alone and submit to Him in Islam. If the pronoun refers to the individual from the people of the Scripture, then the verse means that each one of them will see just before his death what will convince him that Jesus was a true prophet from God, and not God. But that belief at that time will not benefit him, since it comes not out of free choice, but when he sees the angels of punishment.

[20] See verses 5:116-118.

163. Indeed, We have revealed to you (O Muhammad) as We revealed to Noah and the prophets after him. And We revealed to Abraham, Ishmael, Isaac, Jacob, and the prophet-descendants (of Jacob), Jesus, Job, Jonah, Aaron, and Solomon, and We gave the book to David.

164. And messengers We have mentioned to you before, and messengers We have not mentioned to you. And God spoke to Moses (directly).

165. Messengers who gave good news as well as warnings so that humans will have no excuse before God after the messengers (have conveyed the truth). And God is All-Powerful, All-Wise.

166. But (if they reject you O Muhammad, then) God is a Witness that He has revealed it to you, He has sent it down containing knowledge from Him, and the angels are witnesses (too). And God is sufficient as a witness.

167. Indeed, those who disbelieve and block (others) from the way of God have certainly strayed far away.

168. Indeed, those who disbelieve and do wrong, God will not forgive them, nor will He guide them to any path.

169. Except the path to Hell, to stay in it forever. And this is easy for God.[21]

170. O people, the Messenger has come to you with the truth from your Lord, so believe, it is better for you. But if you disbelieve, then to God belongs all that is in the heavens and the earth.[22] And God is All-Knowing, All-Wise.

171. O people of the Scripture, do not go to extremes in your religion, and do not say about God except the truth. The Messiah Jesus, son of Mary, is only a messenger from God and a word from Him, which He sent to Mary, and a soul from Him.[23] So, believe in God and His messengers, and do not say, "Three." Stop, it is better for you. Indeed,

---

[21] No one can oppose Him, and nothing is too difficult for Him.

[22] If you disbelieve, then know that God does not need you, because everything belongs to Him, and all is worshipping Him. And since God has control over everything, know that if you disbelieve, you will not escape His judgment.

[23] Jesus is called a word or a soul from God because he was created when God said, "Be," and he was. In that he is special, because all humans, except Adam and Eve, are created from two parents. But despite his uniqueness, Jesus is like everyone else in that he is not divine, but a mortal creature.

God is one; exalted is He above having a son. To Him belongs whatever is in the heavens and whatever is on the earth. And God is sufficient as a Determiner of all affairs.

172. Never would the Messiah look down upon being a worshipper of God, nor would the angels who are close (to God).[24] And whoever looks down upon the worship of God and is arrogant, then He will gather them to Himself all together.

173. So, for those who believe and do righteous deeds, He will give them their rewards, and add them more out of His bounty. But as for those who look down upon His worship and are arrogant, He will punish them with a painful punishment. And they will not find any protector or helper for themselves other than God.

174. O people, there has come to you a conclusive proof from your Lord, and We have sent down to you a clear light.

---

[24] Everything and everyone else other than God is a worshipper or a servant of God. The verse is asserting that the Messiah would never claim a status above that of a worshipper of God, dismissing any claim to the contrary of his divinity. And indeed he would never disdain such a position, because this is the highest honor any human can aspire to.

175. So, for those who believe in God and hold strong to Him, He will admit them to His mercy and bounty, and guide them to the straight path leading to Him.

CHAPTER 5 *THE TABLE*[25]

14. And We took the covenant from those who said, "We are Christians," but they abandoned part of what they were commanded. So (as a punishment), We planted among them enmity and hatred till the Day of Resurrection. And God will inform them of what they used to do.

15. O people of the Scripture, there has come to you Our Messenger making clear to you much of what you used to hide from the Scripture and overlooking much (of your sins). Indeed, there has come to you from God a light and a clear Book.

16. By which God guides all those who seek His pleasure to safety, and brings them, by His permission, out of darkness into light, and guides them to a straight path.

---

[25] This chapter is named after a miracle of Jesus, when the disciples asked for food to descend upon them from the sky. See verses 5:112-115.

17. Surely, they have disbelieved those who say that God is the Christ, son of Mary. Say, "Who then has the least power against God if He were to destroy the Christ son of Mary, his mother, and everyone on earth?" And God has supreme authority over the heavens and the earth, and whatever is between them. He creates what He wills, and God is Able to do all things.

18. And the Jews and the Christians say, "We are the children of God and His loved ones." Say, "Why then does He punish you for your sins?" Rather, you are only human beings from among those He has created. He forgives whom He wills, and He punishes whom He wills. And God has supreme authority over the heavens and the earth, and whatever is between them, and to Him is the return (of all).

19. O people of the Scripture, Our Messenger has come to you after a suspension of messengers, making (the truth) clear to you, so that you do not say, "No bringer of good news and a warner has come to us." But now a bringer of good news and a warner has come to you. And God is Able to do all things.

44. Indeed, We sent down the Torah, and in it there was guidance and light. By it, the prophets, who were Muslims (in submission to God), judged among the Jews. And so did the godly scholars and the rabbis, for they were entrusted to protect God's Book, and they were witnesses to it (containing God's law). Therefore do not fear people but fear Me, and do not sell My verses for a miserable price. And whoever does not judge by what God has revealed, then those are the disbelievers.

45. And We wrote for them in it a life for a life, an eye for an eye, a nose for a nose, an ear for an ear, a tooth for a tooth, and wounds equal for equal. But whoever forgives, he will be forgiven. And whoever does not judge by what God has revealed, then those are the wrongdoers.

46. And in their (the prophets') footsteps, We sent Jesus the son of Mary, affirming the Torah that had come before him. And We gave him the Gospel, in it was guidance and light, affirming the Torah that had come before it, and a guidance and an admonition for the pious.

47. And let the people of the Gospel judge by what God has revealed in it.[26] And whoever does not

---

[26] Judging by what has been revealed in the Gospel leads invariably to accepting the message of Islam. Jesus has foretold of the coming of a messenger after him (see verse 61:6). And the Gospel, before it had been changed, teaches the same fundamental principles of the Quran.

judge by what God has revealed, then it is those who are the disobedient.

48. And We have revealed to you (O Muhammad) the Book in truth, confirming the Scripture that came before it and a judge over it.[27] So judge between them by what God has revealed, and do not follow their desires away from the truth that has come to you. To each among you, We have given a law and a clear way. And had God willed, He would have made you one nation, but (He intended to) test you with what He has given you, so compete in good deeds.[28] The return of you all is to God, and then He will inform you about what you used to differ.

---

[27] The Quran confirms the truth in the previous books, and corrects the mistakes and alterations in them. The Quran also replaces the laws in the previous books with its laws, and as such, the Quran is a judge over the previous books.

[28] God has given different prophets and their nations different laws to follow, but the fundamentals of all the messages were the same. And God required each nation to submit to the next prophet it receives and to accept the new commands he brings. God had varied the laws because each was most fitting to the time they were revealed in, and it also functioned as a test to see who would submit to the new law of God and who would cling to his customs and the ways of his people. Though humans have not been made into one nation, they are commanded to be just that, by rushing to God's obedience. This is similar to God commanding all to be righteous, but not creating all as such.

49. And so judge between them by what God has revealed and do not follow their desires, but beware of them so that they don't turn you away from some of what God has revealed to you. And if they turn away, then know that God intends to punish them for some of their sins. And indeed, many among people are disobedient.

50. Do they then seek the judgment of Ignorance? And who is better in judgment than God for a people who are certain (in faith).[29]

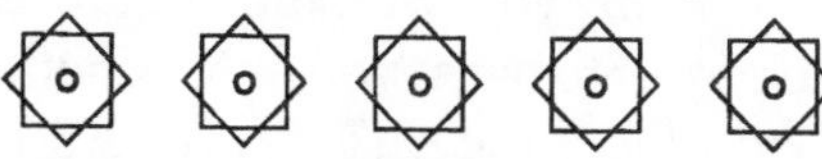

72. Surely, they have disbelieved who say, "God is the Messiah Jesus, son of Mary." But the Messiah said, "O Children of Israel, worship God, my Lord and your Lord. Indeed, whoever sets up partners (in worship) with God, then God has forbidden him Paradise, and the Fire will be his home. And there is none to help the wrongdoers."

73. Surely, disbelievers are those who say, "God is the third of three."[30] But there is no god (that deserves to be worshipped) except One God. And if they do not stop what they are saying, the disbelievers among them will suffer a painful punishment.

---

[29] Leaving the law of God is ignorance, and any law contradicting the law of God is a law of ignorance.

[30] In reference to the Trinity.

74. Will they not repent to God and seek His forgiveness? For God is Oft-Forgiving, Most Merciful.

75. The Messiah son of Mary was only a messenger (like other) messengers that had passed away before him. And his mother was a strong believer.[31] They both used to eat food.[32] Look how We make the proofs clear to them, then look how they turn away.

76. Say, "How do you worship besides God what has no power to harm you or to benefit you? And it is God Who is the All-Hearing, All-Knowing."

77. Say, "O people of the Scripture, do not go beyond the boundaries of the truth (in what you believe), and do not follow the desires of people who had went astray before, had misled many, and had strayed from the straight path."

---

[31] The Arabic word here indicates the highest level of faith possible, where the only one higher is prophethood.

[32] Both the Messiah and his pious mother used to eat, and that is not a characteristic of God, who does not eat nor drink. Also, the one who eats defecates, and this cannot be an attribute of God. Jesus here is likened to all the noble messengers that had preceded him: their message was the same, and their status as non-divine creatures of God is similar. The highest honor that can be afforded to a human is prophethood, and Jesus is one of the five highly regarded prophets. See verse 33:7 & 42:13.

78. Cursed were those who disbelieved among the Children of Israel by the tongue of David and Jesus the son of Mary. That was because they disobeyed and used to transgress.

79. They used not to forbid the evil that each other did. Wicked was what they used to do.

80. You see many of them taking the disbelievers as their close allies. Wicked is what they have earned for their future (in the Hereafter), that God has become angry with them and in the punishment they will stay forever.

81. And had they believed in God, and in the Prophet, and in what has been revealed to him, they would not have taken them as close allies, but many of them are disobedient.

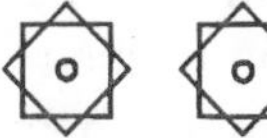    

109. On the Day (of Resurrection), God will gather the messengers and say, "What was the response you received?" They will say, "We have no knowledge. Indeed, only You are the All-Knowing of the unseen."[33]

110. When God will say, "O Jesus, son of Mary, remember My favor upon you and upon your mother when I supported you with the Pure Spirit (Gabriel) and you spoke to people in the cradle and in old age; and when I taught you the Book, wisdom, the Torah and the Gospel; and when you made out of clay the likeness of a bird, by My permission, then you breathed into it, and it became a bird by My permission, and you healed the blind and the leper by My permission, and when you brought the dead to life by My permission; and when I restrained the Children of Israel from (killing) you when you came to them with clear proofs, but the disbelievers among them said, 'This is nothing but plain magic.'

111. And when I put in the hearts of the disciples to believe in Me and My messenger, so they said, "We believe, and bear witness that we are Muslims (in submission to God)."

---

[33] They refer all knowledge back to God, since it is He who knows the sincerity of the hearts and how the people behaved after the prophets died.

112. (And) when the disciples said, "O Jesus, son of Mary, will your Lord send down to us a table spread (with food) from heaven?" He said, "Fear God, if you are indeed believers."

113. They said, "We wish to eat from it and have our hearts be reassured, and to know that you have indeed told us the truth and that we be witnesses to it."

114. Jesus the son of Mary said, "O God, our Lord, send us from heaven a table spread (with food) to be for us a festival for the first of us and the last of us and a sign from You. And provide for us, You are the Best of providers."

115. God said, "I am going to send it down to you, but if any of you after that disbelieves, then I will punish him with a punishment such as I will not put on anyone else."

116. And God will say (on the Day of Resurrection), "O Jesus, son of Mary, did you say to people, 'Worship me and my mother instead of God?'[34]

---

[34] The worship of others with God is the same as worshipping them instead of God. Both mean that worship is directed and given to someone other than God, yet God is the only One who can be worshipped.

" He will say, "Glory be to You! It is not for me to say what I have no right (to say). If I had said it, You would have known it. You know what is (hidden) in myself and I do not know what is in Yours. Indeed, You are the Knower of the unseen.[35]

117. I did not tell them except what You commanded me, 'Worship God, my Lord and your Lord.' And I was a witness over them while I was among them, but when You took me up, You were the Watcher over them, and You are a Witness to all things.

118. If You punish them, they are Your servants, and if You forgive them, indeed You are the All-Mighty, the All-Wise."[36]

---

[35] God, as Jesus said, knows that Jesus did not call for his own worship or his mother's. The aim of the question is to point to those who worship Jesus or Mary that if they were true followers of Jesus, they would stop that practice, because Jesus never called to it. But if they persist, then let them know that Jesus will disown them on the Last Day, and that they have not been following him, but only following their personal preferences.

[36] In other words, You know who is worthy of punishment, so You will punish him. And you know who is worthy of forgiveness, so You will forgive him. For indeed, You are the Mighty who has the power to punish, and You are Wise in dispensing all affairs, so you forgive those who deserve forgiveness.

119. God will say, "This is the Day when the truth will benefit those who were truthful. To them belong gardens with rivers running through it (in Paradise), where they will stay forever. God is pleased with them and they are pleased with Him. That is the great success.

120. To God belongs the heavens and the earth and whatever is within them, and He is Able to do all.

74. And (remember) when Abraham said to his father Azar, "Do you worship idols? Indeed, I see you and your people in clear error."

75. And so we showed Abraham the (signs of our) majesty in the heavens and the earth so that he would be one of those who have certainty (in faith).

76. When the night covered him (with darkness) he saw a star. He said, "This is my lord." But when it set, he said, "I don't like what disappears."

77. And when he saw the moon rising, he said, "This is my lord." But when it set, he said, "Unless my Lord guides me, I will surely be among those who have gone astray."

78. And when he saw the sun rising, he said, "This is my lord. This is greater." But when it set, he said, "O my people, I am indeed free from what you take as partners (in worship with God).

79. Indeed, I have turned (in worship) towards Him who has created the heavens and the earth, leaving away falsehood, and I am not of those who take partners (with God)."

80. And his people argued with him, so he said, "Do you argue with me about God though He has guided me? I do not fear what you associate with Him, (for nothing will happen to me) except what my Lord wills. My Lord has knowledge of all things. Will you not remember?

81. And why would I fear what you associate with Him, and you do not fear that you have associated with God what He has not permitted you (to worship)? So which of the two parties has more right to be secure, if you but know?"

82. Those who believe and do not mix with their belief taking partners with God will have security and they are the guided.

83. And that was Our argument which We gave Abraham against his people. We raise whom We want in degrees. Indeed, your Lord is All--Wise, All--Knowing.

84. And We gave him Isaac and Jacob, each We guided. And Noah, We guided before; and from his progeny, (We guided) David, Solomon, Job, Joseph, Moses, and Aaron. And so do We reward who does good.

85. And (so We guided) Zechariah and John and Jesus and Elijah, all were of the righteous.

86. And (We guided) Ishmael and Elisha and Jonah and Lot, all We preferred above the rest (of their times).

87. And (also We guided some) of their fathers and their progeny and their brothers, and We chose them, and We guided them to a straight path.

88. This is the guidance of God with which He guides whomever He wants from His servants. But if they (the prophets) had taken partners (with God), all that they used to do (of worship) would have been of no benefit to them.

89. Those (prophets) are the ones whom We gave the Book, wisdom, and prophethood to. But if these (disbelievers) reject them, then indeed We have entrusted (the religion and taking care of it) to a people who are not disbelievers in it.

90. Those (prophets) are the ones whom God has guided, so follow their example. Say, "I ask you for no reward for this (message from God). It is only a reminder to all."

91. They did not esteem God and give Him His due when they said, "God did not reveal anything to any human." Say, "Who revealed the Book which Moses brought as light and guidance to people?

You make it into pages so that you can show (some), and conceal many, despite that you were taught what you did not know nor your fathers knew."[37] Say, "God (revealed the Quran)." Then leave them playing in their false talk.

92. And this (Quran) is a blessed Book which We have revealed, confirming (the revelations) that came before it, so that you may warn the Mother of Towns (Mecca) and all those around it. Those who believe in the Hereafter believe in (the Quran), and they are constant in their prayers.

93. And what greater wrong is there than one who fabricates a lie against God, or says, "I have received a revelation," while nothing has been revealed to him; and one who says, "I will reveal like what God has revealed"? And if you could just see the wrong-doers when they are in the agonies of death, while the angels are extending their hands (beating them and saying), "Give out your souls! Today you will be given a humiliating punishment for the lies you used to say against God, and for your arrogance with His verses."

---

[37] How can you do it with all that you know, and how can you repay this favor by hiding it?

94. And truly you have come to Us alone like when We first created you, and you have left behind all that We had given you.[38] And We do not see with you (to help you) your intercessors whom you claimed to be partners with God. (All relations) between you and them have been cut off, and your lies have vanished from you.

---

[38] Like when they were first created, all humans will come to God on the Day of Resurrection with no wealth or property. They will have nothing with them except their good or bad deeds.

CHAPTER 9 *REPENTANCE*

30. And the Jews say, "Ezra is the son of God,"[39] and the Christians say, "The Messiah is the son of God." That is the fabrication of their mouths. They are imitating the claims of the disbelievers of before. May God destroy them, how they turn away (from the truth).

31. They have taken their religious scholars and their monks as lords instead of God (by disobeying God and obeying them), and (they also have taken as their Lord) the Messiah, son of Mary. But they were commanded to worship only one God, none has the right to be worshipped except Him. Exalted is He above what they associate (with Him)."[40]

---

[39] Although not all Jews believed it, they failed to condemn it (see verses 5:78-79). When a sin is allowed to persist and spread unopposed, the whole community becomes liable.

[40] The religious scholars are the ones possessing knowledge, and the monks are the ones immersed in ritual and worship. Both are considered religious leaders and examples, and through their influence they can lead people astray.

32. They want to put out God's light with their mouths, but God refuses except that He completes His light although the disbelievers hate it.[41]

33. It is He Who has sent His Messenger (Muhammad) with guidance and the true religion, to make it superior over all religions despite the hatred of those who associate others with God.[42]

34. O you who believe, indeed many religious scholars and monks eat away people's wealth unjustly, and turn (others) away from the way to God. And those who treasure gold and silver, and do not spend it in the Way of God, then give them the news of a painful punishment.

35. On the Day when it will be heated in the Fire of Hell and their foreheads, their sides, and their backs will be burned with it, (and it will be said), "This is what you treasured for yourselves, so taste what you used to treasure."

---

[41] Opposing God is like one blowing with his mouth to extinguish the light of the sun.

[42] The intrinsic superiority of the religion lies in the truth it has, where it is superior in proofs and signs before all to see. Any other religion or ideology will fall short in comparison.

CHAPTER 19 *MARY*

2. This is the mention of the mercy of your Lord to His servant Zechariah.

3. When he called upon his Lord in secret.

4. He said, "My Lord, Indeed my bones have grown weak, and gray hair has overtaken my head, and you have never turned me down when I asked You, O my Lord.

5. "And indeed, I fear (what) my relatives (will do) after me, and my wife is barren. So grant me from You an heir,

6. "Who will inherit me and inherit the family of Jacob. And make him, my Lord, pleasing (to You and your servants)."[43]

---

[43] Zechariah worried how his relatives will behave and if they will continue to obey God after his death, so he prayed for a son who would be a prophet to carry on his work and take care of his family. The inheritance he speaks of is that of religious knowledge and prophethood, not wealth.

7. "O Zechariah, indeed We give you the good news of a son, whose name will be John. We have not made someone like him before."[44]

8. He said, "My Lord, how can I have a son, when my wife is barren, and I have reached extreme old age?"

9. (The angel) said, "So said your Lord, 'It is easy for Me, for I have created you before, and you were nothing.'"

10. (Zechariah) said, "My Lord, give me a sign." He said, "Your sign is that you will not be able speak to people for three nights, though you are healthy."

11. Then he came out to his people from the prayer room, and signaled to them to praise (God) in the morning and in the afternoon.

12. (God said), "O John, hold strong to the Scripture (the Torah)." And We gave him prophethood as a child.

13. And We made him soft-hearted (towards others), and pure, and he was fearing of God,

14. And dutiful to his parents, and he was not arrogant or disobedient (to God or to his parents).

---

[44] One way John was unique was that God had made him a prophet when he was still a child (see verse 19:12).

15. And peace be on him the day he was born, the day he dies, and the day he will be raised alive.

16. And mention in the Book (the story of) Mary, when she withdrew from her family to an eastern place.

17. And she placed a screen to seclude herself from them. Then We sent to her Our angel (Gabriel), and he took the form of a well-created man before her.

18. She said, "Indeed I seek refuge with the Most Merciful from you, if you do fear God."[45]

19. (The angel) said, "I am only the messenger of your Lord to give to you (the news of) a pure boy."

20. She said, "How can I have a son, when no man has touched me (in marriage), and I am not a prostitute?"

21. He said, "So your Lord said, 'It is easy for Me. And We will make him a sign to people and a mercy from Us. And it is a matter (already) decided.' "[46]

---

[45] The Most Merciful is one of the names of God in the Quran.

[46] Jesus is a sign of God's power, where God showed people that He could create Jesus without a father, as He created Adam without any parents. Jesus is also a sign that God is well able to resurrect all people after their death, since the one who creates from nothing is quite able to bring back to life.

22. So she conceived him, and she withdrew with him to a remote place.

23. And the pains of childbirth drove her to the trunk of a date tree. She said, "I wish I had died before this, and had been long forgotten."

24. Then (baby Jesus) called her from below her, saying, "Don't be sad. Your Lord has provided a stream under you.

25. Shake the trunk of the date tree towards you, and it will drop on you fresh ripe dates.

26. So eat and drink and be happy. And if you see any human, then say, 'Indeed I have vowed a fast to the Most Merciful so I will not speak to any human today.'"

27. Then she carried him and brought him to her people. They said, "O Mary, indeed you have done a great evil."

28. "O sister of Aaron, your father was not an evil man, and your mother was not a prostitute."

29. So she pointed to him. They said, "How can we speak to a child in the cradle?"

30. (Jesus) said, "Indeed, I am a servant of God. He has given me the Scripture and made me a prophet.[47]

31. And He has made me blessed wherever I am, and has commanded me to me pray and give charity as long as I remain alive.

32. And (has made) me kind to my mother, and did not make me arrogant or miserable.

33. And peace be upon me the day I was born, and the day I will die, and the day I will be raised alive."

34. This is Jesus, the son of Mary. And this is the statement of truth, which they doubt.

35. It is not possible for God to take a son. Far is He above this! When He decides something, He just says to it, "Be," and it is.[48]

---

[47] Prophethood is the highest and most honorable position a human can reach. A prophet is one who receives revelations from God through Angel Gabriel. A messenger is a prophet who receives a book from God, as well as laws to convey to his people. Jesus attained the highest honor by being both a prophet and a messenger.

[48] If the creation of Jesus without a father makes him the son of God, then everything created like Jesus without a predecessor should be divine too, and that includes Adam, Eve, the first animals, and this whole earth with its mountains and waters. But Jesus was created like all things on this earth, when God said, "Be," and he was.

36. (Jesus said), "And indeed God is my Lord and your Lord, so worship Him. That is a straight path."

37. But the sects disagreed (over the straight path), so woe to the disbelievers from meeting a horrible Day.

38. How clearly will they see and hear on the Day when they will appear before Us. Yet the wrongdoers today are in clear error.[49]

39. And warn them about the Day of Regret[50], when all things will be settled, yet (still) they are unaware, and they do not believe.

40. It is We who will inherit the earth and whoever is on it, and to Us they will return.

---

[49] On the Day of Judgment there will be no excuse left for the disbelievers, and the veil they used to cover their eyes with will be no more. They will have no choice then but to admit to the truth they were denying in this world, but it will be too late for them.

[50] One of the names of the Last Day.

CHAPTER 21 *THE PROPHETS*

72. And We gave to Abraham Isaac, and also Jacob. And We made each righteous.

73. And We made them examples, guiding (others) by Our revelation. And We inspired them to do good, to perform prayer, and to give charity. And they worshipped Us alone.

74. And We made Lot a prophet and gave him knowledge, and saved him from the city that was committing evil deeds. Indeed, they were wicked and disobedient people.

75. And We brought him to Our Mercy. Truly, he was of the righteous.

76. And Noah, when he prayed before, We answered his prayer and saved him and his family from the great distress (the flood).

77. And We helped him against the people who denied Our revelations. They were an evil people, so We drowned them all.

78. And David and Solomon, when they judged in the case of the people's sheep that had grazed at night in the field. And We were witness to their judgment.

79. And We gave its understanding to Solomon,[51] and We made both prophets and gave knowledge to. And We commanded the mountains and the birds to glorify Us along with David. And We are able to do (all).

80. And We taught him the making of metal coats of armor to protect you in your battles. So are you then grateful?

81. And We brought the strong wind under Solomon's control, running when he wishes towards the land that We had blessed (Palestine). And We are All-Knowing of all things.

82. And from the devils were some who dived (the seas) for him and did some other work. And it was We Who controlled them.

---

[51] The case involved the sheep of one party destroying the field of another at night. David's ruling was for the sheep to be surrendered to the owners of the field as compensation for the damage. Solomon's ruling was that the sheep should be handed temporarily to the field owners to benefit from them, while the sheep owners restore the field. Once the field is restored to the way it was, the sheep would go back to its owners.

83. And Job when he prayed to his Lord, "Indeed, harm has touched me, and You are the Most Merciful of all the merciful."

84. So We answered his prayer and removed his harm. And We restored his family to him and doubled their numbers out of mercy from Us and a reminder to the worshippers.

85. And Ishmael, and Enoch and Dhul Kifl, all were patient.

86. And We brought them into Our Mercy. Indeed, they were of the righteous.

87. And Jonah, when he went off in anger, and thought that We will not punish him. And he prayed in the darkness (inside the whale), "None has the right to be worshipped but You, glorified are You. Truly, I have been of the wrongdoers."

88. So We answered his prayer, and saved him from distress. And so We save the believers.

89. And Zechariah, when he prayed to his Lord, "O My Lord, do not leave me alone childless, and You are the best of inheritors."

90. So We answered his prayer and gave him John, and cured his wife (to bear children) for him. For they used to rush to do good, and used to pray to Us with hope and fear, and they were humble before Us.

91. And she who guarded her chastity, so We breathed (a spirit) into her through Our angel, and We made her and her son (Jesus) a sign for the worlds.

92. Indeed, the religion of your prophets is one religion, and I am your Lord, so worship Me.[52]

---

[52] The religion of all the prophets of God is one religion, calling to the worship of the One God and to the same virtues. So, if God is one, and the religion is one, why do you differ and separate?

CHAPTER 23 *THE BELIEVERS*

23. And We sent Noah to his people, and he said, "My people, worship God, for you have no other God but Him. Are you not afraid (of His punishment)?"

24. Yet the leaders of the disbelievers from his people said, "He is only a human like you, seeking to be better than you. If God had wanted, He would have sent down angels (as prophets). We have not heard such talk from our fathers before.

25. He is only a madman, so wait a while (to see what happens) with him."

26. (Noah) said, "O my Lord, they have denied me so help me."

27. So We revealed to him, "Build the ship under Our (watchful) Eye and guidance. Then, when Our punishment comes, and (even) the clay ovens spring water, take into it from each (creature) a pair, and your family except for those who have deserved the punishment. And do not talk to Me about (saving) those who have done wrong. They will be drowned.

28. And when you and whoever is with you have boarded the ship, then say, "Praise be to God, who has saved us from the wrongdoers."

29. And say, "My Lord, let me land at a blessed landing-place, for You are the best of those who bring to land."

30. Indeed, there are signs in this (story), and we test (the people with the prophets we send to them).

31. Then We created another generation after them.

32. And We sent to them a messenger from them (saying), "Worship God, for you have no other God but Him. Are you not afraid (of His punishment)?"

33. Yet the leaders of his people, who have disbelieved and denied the Hereafter and We have given plenty to in this life, said, "He is only a human like you. He eats from you eat, and drinks from what you drink.

34. And if you were to obey a human like you, indeed you would be losers.

35. Does he promise you that when you die and turn into dust and bones that you will be resurrected?

36. What you are promised is unbelievable.

37. There is nothing more than our life in this world. We die and we live. And we are not going to be resurrected.

38. He is only a man who has fabricated a lie against God, and we are not going to believe him."

39. He said, "O my Lord, they rejected me, so help me."

40. (God) said, "Soon they will be sorry."

41. So The Cry rightfully overtook them, and We made them as if they are dead plants. So away with the wrongdoers.[53]

42. Then We created other generations after them.

43. Every nation has an appointed end that it does not escape.

44. Then We sent Our messengers one after the other. Every time a messenger came to his nation, they denied him, so We destroyed them one after the other, and We made them into stories.[54] So away with a people who don't believe.

45. Then We sent Moses and his brother Aaron with Our miracles and clear signs,

46. To Pharaoh and his ruling elites, but they were proud and arrogant.

---

[53] The Cry is a punishment that comes from the sky with complete destruction.

[54] God destroyed them and turned them into mere stories, which are repeated because of their strange events and lessons.

47. They said, "Should we believe two men like us, and their people are our servants."

48. So they denied them and they were destroyed.

49. And We gave Moses the Scripture so that they be guided.

50. And We made the son of Mary and his mother a sign, And We gave them refuge and rest on a high ground with flowing water.[55]

51. O messengers, eat from the lawful foods and do good deeds. Indeed, I know what you do.

52. And your religion (O prophets) is one religion, and I am your Lord, so keep your duty to Me.

53. But they (the people) have broken their religion between them into pieces, each group happy with what it has.[56]

54. So leave them in their ignorance until the time (of punishment).

---

[55] This is where Mary gave birth to Jesus.

[56] After God's command to His prophets and their nations to follow the one religion He revealed, the people broke it up into parts and divided into sects. Each sect holds to one part of their book and religion and ignores the rest, claiming that the other faction is misguided. God commanded unity, but it is people who ignored His command and divided.

55. Do they think that We increase them in wealth and children,

56. Because (We) are rushing good things to them? No, but they do not perceive.[57]

57. Indeed, those who are afraid of their Lord's punishment,

58. And those who believe in the revelations of their Lord,

59. And those who do not take partners with their Lord,

60. And those who give what they give while their hearts are fearful, because they are returning to their Lord,[58]

61. It is those who rush to do good deeds, and they are first in them.

---

[57] The material wealth heaped on them, despite their disobedience, is not a sign of God's favor, but a sign of His anger. He gives them this wealth after they have rejected the truth, so they continue headlong with their evil deeds until the punishment of God comes.

[58] They do good and give charity, but are afraid that it is not good enough to be accepted from them. At the same time, they hope that God's Mercy would grant them heaven. This attitude of theirs protects them from self-conceit, and makes them ever dependent on God. They keep performing good deeds because they never think that they have done enough, but they know that it is God's Mercy, and not their deeds, that is going to save them.

62. And We do not put on any soul more than it can bear. And We have a record (of everyone's deeds) which speaks the truth, and they will not be wronged.

CHAPTER 33 *THE GROUPS*

7. And (remember) when We took from the prophets their covenant (to convey and follow the truth), and We took it from you (O Muhammad), and from Noah, Abraham, Moses, and Jesus son of Mary.[59] And we took from them a firm covenant,

8. So that He may ask the truthful (prophets) about their truth (which they conveyed). And He has prepared for the disbelievers a painful punishment.[60]

---

[59] The five prophets mentioned here are the best among all the prophets. Their noted position is repeated in verse 42:13. They are called the messengers of strong will and determination, as in verse 46:35.

[60] God will ask the prophets whether the nations had accepted the message or not, and then He will reward and punish the people accordingly. The question is not because God does not know who has believed and who has not, but to vindicate the prophets and champion them on that day, and to show the people how much they have gained by following the prophets, or how much they have lost if they did not.

CHAPTER 42 *THE CONSULTATION*

13. He (God) has given you the same religion that He commanded Noah with, and what We have revealed to you (O Muhammad), and what We commanded Abraham with, and Moses and Jesus that you should establish the religion, and not be divided in it. But what you call to is difficult for those who associate others with God. God brings closer to Himself whom He wills, and guides to Himself who turns to Him.[61]

14. Yet they divided after the knowledge had come to them out of transgression against each other.[62] And if not for a previous word from your Lord (to postpone punishment) till a designated time, judgment would have been given between them. And indeed, those who inherited the Scripture after them are in great doubt about it.

---

[61] The prohibition of dividing the religion is a prohibition against following some of it and rejecting the rest, which would divide the followers of the prophets into groups and sects. Following the revealed religion of the prophets is the basis of unity in this world.

[62] They transgressed because of envy, animosity, and competition for material gains.

15. So call to this (religion of the prophets), and stay straight as you were commanded, and do not follow their desires but say, "I believe in all the Scripture that God revealed, and I am commanded to be just with you. God is our Lord and your Lord, and we have our deeds and you have yours. There is no argument between us and you (after the truth has been made clear). God will gather us (for judgment on the Last Day), and to Him is the return."

16. And those who argue about God (to turn people away from Him), after (the believers) have accepted Him, their argument is false before their Lord, and on them is (His) anger, and there will be a severe punishment for them.[63]

---

[63] Those who attempt to turn people away from God after God's signs and verses have been made clear to people and they accepted them, will find that their attempts and arguments will earn them only God's anger and punishment.

CHAPTER 43 *THE ORNAMENT*

57. And when the son of Mary was compared (to their idols), your people cried out (overjoyed).

58. And said, "Are our gods better or is he?" They did not present the comparison except to argue. They are a quarreling people.[64]

59. He (Jesus) was only a servant whom We have favored, and We made him an example to the Children of Israel.

60. And if We want, We could [destroy all of you, and] replace you with angels on earth (to worship Me).

---

[64] When disputing with Prophet Muhammad, the polytheists compared their idols to Jesus. They argued that, if as the Quran stated, they and their idols will be in Hellfire, then the same holds true for Jesus and those who worshipped him, so how can the Quran praise Jesus? They made that comparison despite knowing that the Quran has praised Jesus as a prophet who called to God and not to his own worship, while their idols are inanimate rocks and stones that will be thrown in Hellfire to show the polytheists the reality of what they were worshipping.

61. And he (Jesus) is a sign of (the coming of) the Hour, so do not doubt it.[65] And follow Me, this is a straight path (leading to God and His paradise).

62. And do not let Satan prevent you (from following Me). Indeed, he is a clear enemy to you.

63. And when Jesus came with clear proofs, he said, "I have come to you with prophethood, and to make clear to you some of what you disagree about, so fear God and obey me.

64. Indeed, God is my Lord and your Lord, so worship Him. This is a straight path."

65. But the groups disagreed among themselves (about the message of Jesus), so woe to those who disbelieved from the punishment of a painful Day.

66. Are they waiting except for the (punishment of the) Hour to suddenly come upon them while they do not know?

67. On that Day, close friends will be enemies to each other, except for the pious.

---

[65] The second coming of Jesus will be a sign that the Day of Judgment is near.

68. (God will say to the pious), "My servants, there is no fear or sorrow for you today,

69. (You) who believed in Our verses and were Muslims (submitting to God)."

CHAPTER 57 *THE IRON*

26. And indeed, We sent Noah and Abraham, and put prophethood and scripture in their offspring. Yet only some of them were guided, and many of them were disobedient.

27. Then We sent after them Our messengers, and We sent Jesus son of Mary, and gave him the Gospel. And We put in the hearts of those who followed him compassion and mercy. But We did not command monasticism, rather they invented it for themselves to please God with it, yet they did not observe it as it should be observed. So We gave those who believed among them their reward, but many of them are disobedient.

28. O you who believe, fear God and believe in His messenger, He will then give you a double portion of His mercy, and give you light by which you can walk, and He will forgive you. And God is Most Forgiving, Most Merciful.

29. (This We say) so that the people of the Scripture may know that they have no control over God's favor, and that (His) favor is in His Hand to give it to whomever He wills. And God is the Owner of great bounty.[66]

---

[66] God gives guidance to whomever He wills, regardless of background and race. And when people believe, God honors them and lifts higher than everyone else. But when they disbelieve, God demotes them even though before they might have been honorable.

CHAPTER 61 *THE ROWS*

1. Whatever is in the heavens and whatever is on the earth glorifies God. And He is the All-Mighty, the All-Wise.

2. O you who believe, why do you say what you do not do?

3. It is most hateful to God that you say what you do not do.

4. Indeed, God loves those who fight in His cause in rows as if they were a solid structure.

5. And (remember) when Moses said to his people, "O my people, why do you harm me while you know that I am the messenger of God to you?" So when they turned away (from obeying God), God turned their hearts away (from the truth). And God does not guide the disobedient people.

6. And (remember) when Jesus, son of Mary, said, "O Children of Israel, I am the messenger of God to you confirming the Torah that came before me, and bringing good news of a messenger that will come after me, whose his name will be Ahmed.[67] But when he came to them with clear proofs, they said, "This is clear magic."[68]

7. And what greater wrong is there than one who fabricates a lie against God, though he is being invited to Islam? And God does not guide the wrongdoers.[69]

8. They want to put out God's light with their mouths, but God will complete His light although the disbelievers hate it.

9. It is He is who has sent His messenger with guidance and the religion of truth to make it superior over all religions even though those who associate others with God hate it.

---

[67] This is another name for Prophet Muhammad.

[68] This can refer to both prophets, Jesus and Muhammad, peace be upon them. When they came with the message from God to their people, they were accused of bringing magic.

[69] When the prophets come to them with God's message, they deny it and accuse their prophets with all sorts of accusations, though they should be grateful that God has sent them clear guidance on the hands of the noblest men. That is why this is the greatest crime one can commit.

10. O you who believe, shall I guide you to a business that will save you from a painful punishment?

11. You believe in God and His messenger, and strive in the cause of God with your wealth and your lives. That will be better for you, if you but know.[70]

12. (If you do so), He will forgive your sins, and admit you into gardens with running rivers under them, and into pleasant houses in Gardens of Eternity.[71] That is indeed the great success.

13. And (He will give you) another (blessing) that you love, help from God and a quick victory. And give good news to the believers.

---

[70] Doing good and earning Heaven is likened to a business transaction. Because each human desires profit and invests much of his life pursuing it, God here is directing to the most profitable of transactions. It should be noted that all the good deeds combined are not sufficient in themselves for one to earn Heaven, they merely earn one God's Mercy, and it is God's Mercy that admits people into Heaven.

[71] "Gardens of Eternity" is one of the names of Paradise in the Quran.

14. O you who believe, champion God's (religion), like when Jesus son of Mary said to the disciples, "Who will champion God's (religion) with me?" The disciples said, "We are the champions of God's (religion)." Then a group of the Children of Israel believed and a group disbelieved. So We supported those who believed against their enemy, and they became victorious.[72]

---

[72] The victory of the believers came through the message of Islam, and it was a physical and a spiritual victory. Islam removed all doubt about Jesus and offered conclusive proofs of his prophethood, and that was the spiritual victory. Islam also physically spread, which gave the believers in the message of Jesus refuge and power against their enemy, and that was the physical victory.

CHAPTER 66 *THE PROHIBITION*

10. God gives as an example for those who disbelieve, the wife of Noah and the wife of Lot. They were married to two of our righteous servants, but they betrayed them (by disbelieving), so they (Noah and Lot) did not help them with God, and it was said, "Enter the Fire along with those who enter."

11. And God gives as an example for those who believe, the wife of Pharaoh, when she said, "My Lord, build for me a home near You in paradise, and save me from Pharaoh and his deeds, and save me from the wrongdoing people.

12. And (the example of) Mary, the daughter of Imran, who guarded her chastity, so We blew (the spirit of Jesus) into her through Our angel (Gabriel). And she believed in the words of her Lord, and His scriptures, and she was of the devout ones.